CONFESSIONS OF
A SINNER

SAINT AUGUSTINE

CONFESSIONS OF A SINNER

TRANSLATED BY R. S. PINE-COFFIN

PENGUIN BOOKS

PENGUIN BOOKS
Published by the Penguin Group
Penguin Books USA Inc., 375 Hudson Street,
New York, New York 10014, U.S.A.
Penguin Books Ltd, 27 Wrights Lane,
London W8 5TZ, England
Penguin Books Australia Ltd, Ringwood,
Victoria, Australia
Penguin Books Canada Ltd, 10 Alcorn Avenue,
Toronto, Ontario, Canada M4V 3B2
Penguin Books (N.Z.) Ltd, 182–190 Wairau Road,
Auckland 10, New Zealand

Penguin Books Ltd, Registered Offices:
Harmondsworth, Middlesex, England

Published in Penguin Books 1995

This selection is from R. S. Pine-Coffin's translation
of *Confessions*, published by Penguin Books.

ISBN 0 14 60.0203 2

Printed in the United States of America

CONFESSIONS OF
A SINNER

Book I

1

Can any praise be worthy of the Lord's majesty? How magnificent his strength! How inscrutable his wisdom! Man is one of your creatures, Lord, and his instinct is to praise you. He bears about him the mark of death, the sign of his own sin, to remind him that you thwart the proud. But still, since he is a part of your creation, he wishes to praise you. The thought of you stirs him so deeply that he cannot be content unless he praises you, because you made us for yourself and our hearts find no peace until they rest in you.

Grant me, Lord, to know and understand whether a man is first to pray to you for help or to praise you, and whether he must know you before he can call you to his aid. If he does not know you, how can he pray to you? For he may call for some other help, mistaking it for yours.

Or are men to pray to you and learn to know you through their prayers? Only, how are they to call upon the Lord until they have learned to believe in him? And how are they to believe in him without a preacher to listen to?

Those who look for the Lord will cry out in praise of him, because all who look for him shall find him, and when they find him they will praise him. I shall look for you, Lord, by praying to you and as I pray I shall believe in you, because we have had preachers to tell us about you. It is my faith that calls to you, Lord, the faith which you gave me and made to live in me through the merits of your Son, who became man, and through the ministry of your preacher.

2

How shall I call upon my God for aid, when the call I make is for my Lord and my God to come into myself? What place is there in me to which my God can come, what place that can receive the God who made heaven and earth? Does this then mean, O Lord my God, that there is in me something fit to contain you? Can even heaven and earth, which you made and in which you made me, contain you? Or, since nothing that exists could exist without you, does this mean that whatever exists does, in this sense, contain you? If this is so, since I too exist, why do I ask you to come into me? For I should not be there at all unless, in this way, you were already present within me. I am not in hell, and yet you are there too, for if I sink down to the world beneath, you are present still. So, then, I should be null and void and could not exist at all, if you, my God, were not in me.

Or is it rather that I should not exist, unless I existed in you? For all things find in you their origin, their impulse, the centre of their being. This, Lord, is the true answer to my question. But if I exist in you, how can I call upon you to come to me? And where would you come from? For you, my God, have said that you fill heaven and earth, but I cannot go beyond the bounds of heaven and earth so that you may leave them to come to me.

3

Do heaven and earth, then, contain the whole of you, since you fill them? Or, when once you have filled them, is some part of you left over because they are too small to hold you? If this is so, when you have filled heaven and earth, does that part of you which remains flow over into some other place? Or is it that you have no need to be contained in anything, because you contain all things in yourself and fill them by reason of the very fact that you contain them? For the things which you fill by containing them do not sustain and support you as a water-vessel supports the liquid which fills it. Even if they were broken to pieces, you would not flow out of them and away. And when you pour yourself out over us, you are not drawn down to us but draw us up to yourself: you are not scattered away, but you gather us together.

You fill all things, but do you fill them with your whole self? Or is it that the whole of creation is too small to hold you and therefore holds only a part of you? And is this same part of you present in all things at once, or do different things contain different parts of you, greater or smaller according to their size? Does this mean that one part of you is greater and another smaller? Or are you present entirely everywhere at once, and no single thing contains the whole of you?

4

What, then, is the God I worship? He can be none but the Lord God himself, for who but the Lord is God? What other refuge can there be, except our God? You, my God, are supreme, utmost in goodness, mightiest and all-powerful, most merciful and most just. You are the most hidden from us and yet the most present amongst us, the most beautiful and yet the most strong, ever enduring and yet we cannot comprehend you. You are unchangeable and yet you change all things. You are never new, never old, and yet all things have new life from you. You are the unseen power that brings decline upon the proud. You are ever active, yet always at rest. You gather all things to yourself, though you suffer no need. You support, you fill, and you protect all things. You create them, nourish them, and bring them to perfection. You seek to make them your own, though you lack for nothing. You love your creatures, but with a gentle love. You treasure them, but without apprehension. You grieve for wrong, but suffer no pain. You can be angry and yet serene. Your works are varied, but your purpose is one and the same. You welcome all who come to you, though you never lost them. You are never in need yet are glad to gain, never covetous yet you exact a return for your gifts. We give abundantly to you so that we may deserve a reward; yet which of us has anything that does not come from you? You repay us what we deserve, and yet you owe nothing to any. You release us from our debts, but you lose nothing thereby. You are my God, my Life, my holy Delight, but is this enough to say of you? Can any man say enough when he speaks of you? Yet woe betide those who are silent about you! For even those who are most gifted with speech cannot find words to describe you.

Who will grant me to rest content in you? To whom shall I turn for the gift of your coming into my heart and filling it to the brim, so that I may forget all the wrong I have done and embrace you alone, my only source of good?

Why do you mean so much to me? Help me to find words to explain. Why do I mean so much to you, that you should command me to love you? And if I fail to love you, you are angry and threaten me with great sorrow, as if not to love you were not sorrow enough in itself. Have pity on me and help me, O Lord my God. Tell me why you mean so much to me. Whisper in my heart, I am here to save you. Speak so that I may hear your words. My heart has ears ready to listen to you, Lord. Open them wide and whisper in my heart, I am here to save you. I shall hear your voice and make haste to clasp you to myself. Do not hide your face away from me, for I would gladly meet my death to see it, since not to see it would be death indeed.

My soul is like a house, small for you to enter, but I pray you to enlarge it. It is in ruins, but I ask you to remake it. It contains much that you will not be pleased to see: this I know and do not hide. But who is to rid it of these things? There is no one but you to whom I can say: if I have sinned unwittingly, do you absolve me. Keep me ever your own servant, far from pride. I trust, and trusting I find words to utter. Lord, you know that this is true. For have I not made my transgression known to you? Did you not remit the guilt of my sin? I do not wrangle with you for judgement, for you are Truth itself, and I have no wish to delude myself, for fear that my malice should be self-betrayed. No, I do not wrangle with you, for, if you, Lord, will keep record of our iniquities, Master, who has strength to bear it?

6

But, dust and ashes though I am, let me appeal to your pity, since it is to you in your mercy that I speak, not to a man, who would simply laugh at me. Perhaps you too may laugh at me, but you will relent and have pity on me. For all I want to tell you, Lord, is that I do not know where I came from when I was born into this life which leads to death—or should I say, this death which leads to life? This much is hidden from me. But, although I do not remember it all myself, I know that when I came into the world all the comforts which your mercy provides were there ready for me. This I was told by my parents, the father who begat me and the mother who conceived me, the two from whose bodies you formed me in the limits of time. So it was that I was given the comfort of woman's milk.

But neither my mother nor my nurses filled their breasts of their own accord, for it was you who used them, as your law prescribes, to give me infant's food and a share of the riches which you distribute even among the very humblest of all created things. It was also by your gift that I did not wish for more than you gave, and that my nurses gladly passed on to me what you gave to them. They did this because they loved me in the way that you had ordained, and their love made them anxious to give to me what they had received in plenty from you. For it was to their own good that what was good for me should come to me from them; though, of course, it did not come to me from them but, through them, from you, because you, my God, are the source of all good and everywhere you preserve me. All this I have learned since then, because all the gifts you have given to me, both spiritual and material, proclaim the truth of it. But in those days all I knew was how to suck, and how to lie still when my body sensed comfort or cry when it felt pain.

Later on I began to smile as well, first in my sleep, and then when I was awake. Others told me this about myself, and I believe what they said, because we see other babies do the same. But I cannot remember it myself. Little by little I began to realize where I was and to want to make my wishes known to others, who might satisfy them. But this I could not do, because my wishes were inside me, while other people were outside, and they had no faculty which could penetrate my mind. So I would toss my arms and legs about and make noises, hoping that such few signs as I could make would show my meaning, though they were quite unlike what they were meant to mime. And if my wishes were not carried out, either because they had not been understood or because what I wanted would have harmed me, I would get cross with my elders, who were not at my beck and call, and with people who were not my servants, simply because they did not attend to my wishes; and I would take my revenge by bursting into tears. By watching babies I have learnt that this is how they behave, and they, quite unconsciously, have done more than those who brought me up and knew all about it to convince me that I behaved in just the same way myself.

My infancy is long since dead, yet I am still alive. But you, Lord, live for ever and nothing in you dies, because you have existed from before the very beginning of the ages, before anything that could be said to go before, and you are God and Lord of all you have created. In you are the first causes of all things not eternal, the unchangeable origins of all things that suffer change, the everlasting reason of all things that are subject to the passage of time and have no reason in themselves. Have pity, then, on me, O God, for it is pity that I need. Answer my prayer and tell me whether my infancy followed upon some other stage of life that died before it. Was it the stage of life that I spent in my mother's womb? For I have learnt a little about that too, and I have myself seen women who were pregnant. But what came before that, O God my Delight? Was I anywhere? Was I anybody? These are questions I must put to you, for I have no one else to answer them. Neither my father nor my mother could tell me, nor could I find out from the experience of other people or from my own memory. Do my questions provoke you to smile at me and bid me simply to acknowledge you and praise you for what I do know?

I do acknowledge you, Lord of heaven and earth, and I praise you for my first beginnings, although I cannot remember them. But you have allowed men to discover these things about themselves by watching other babies, and also to learn much from what women have to tell. I know that I was a living person even at that age, and as I came towards the end of infancy I tried to find signs to convey my feelings to others. Where could such a living creature come from if not from you, O Lord? Can it be that any man has skill to fabricate himself? Or can there be some channel by which we derive our life and our very existence from some other source than you? Surely we can only derive them from our Maker, from you, Lord, to whom living and being are not different things, since infinite life and infinite being are one and the same. For you are infinite and never change. In you 'today' never comes to an end: and yet our 'today' does come to an end in you, because time, as well as everything else, exists in you. If it did not, it would have no means of passing. And since your years never come to an end, for you they are simply 'today'. The countless days of our lives and of our forefathers' lives have passed by within your 'today'. From it they have received their due measure of duration and their very existence. And so it will be with all the other days which are still to come. But you yourself are eternally the same. In your 'today' you will make all that is to exist tomorrow and thereafter, and in your 'today' you have made all that existed yesterday and for ever before.

Need it concern me if some people cannot understand this? Let them ask what it means, and be glad to ask: but they may content themselves with the question alone. For it is better for them to find you and leave the question unanswered than to find the answer without finding you.

7

Hear me, O God! How wicked are the sins of men! Men say this and you pity them, because you made man, but you did not make sin in him.

Who can recall to me the sins I committed as a baby? For in your sight no man is free from sin, not even a child who has lived only one day on earth. Who can show me what my sins were? Some small baby in whom I can see all that I do not remember about myself? What sins, then, did I commit when I was a baby myself? Was it a sin to cry when I wanted to feed at the breast? I am too old now to feed on mother's milk, but if I were to cry for the kind of food suited to my age, others would rightly laugh me to scorn and remonstrate with me. So then too I deserved a scolding for what I did; but since I could not have understood the scolding, it would have been unreasonable, and most unusual, to rebuke me. We root out these faults and discard them as we grow up, and this is proof enough that they are faults, because I have never seen a man purposely throw out the good when he clears away the bad. It can hardly be right for a child, even at that age, to cry for everything, including things which would harm him; to work himself into a tantrum against people older than himself and not required to obey him; and to try his best to strike and hurt others who know better than he does, including his own parents, when they do not give in to him and refuse to pander to whims which would only do him harm. This shows that, if babies are innocent, it is not for lack of will to do harm, but for lack of strength.

I have myself seen jealousy in a baby and know what it means. He was not old enough to talk, but whenever he saw his foster-brother at the breast, he would grow pale with envy. This much is common knowledge. Mothers and nurses say that they can work such things out of the system by one means or another, but surely it cannot be called innocence, when the milk flows in such abundance from its source, to object to a rival desperately in need and depending for his life on this one form of nourishment? Such faults are not small or unimportant, but we are tender-hearted and bear with them because we know that the child will grow out of them. It is clear that they are not mere peccadilloes, because the same faults are intolerable in older persons.

You, O Lord my God, gave me my life and my body when I was born. You gave my body its five senses; you furnished it with limbs and gave it its proper proportions; and you implanted in it all the instincts necessary for the welfare and safety of a living creature. For these gifts you command me to acknowledge you and praise you and sing in honour of your name, because you are Almighty God, because you are good, and because I owe you praise for these things, even if you had done nothing else. No one but you can do these things, because you are the one and only mould in which all things are cast and the perfect form which shapes all things, and everything takes its place according to your law.

I do not remember that early part of my life, O Lord, but I believe what other people have told me about it and from watching other babies I can conclude that I also lived as they do. But, true though my conclusions may be, I do not like to think of that period as part of the same life I now lead, because it is dim and forgotten and, in this sense, it is no different from the time I spent in my mother's womb. But if I was born in sin and guilt was with me already when my mother conceived me, where, I ask you, Lord, where or when was I, your servant, ever innocent? But I will say no more about that time, for since no trace of it remains in my memory, it need no longer concern me.

8

The next stage in my life, as I grew up, was boyhood. Or would it be truer to say that boyhood overtook me and followed upon my infancy—not that my infancy left me, for, if it did, where did it go? All the same, it was no longer there, because I ceased to be a baby unable to talk, and was now a boy with the power of speech. I can remember that time, and later on I realized how I had learnt to speak. It was not my elders who showed me the words by some set system of instruction, in the way that they taught me to read not long afterwards; but, instead, I taught myself by using the intelligence which you, my God, gave to me. For when I tried to express my meaning by crying out and making various sounds and movements, so that my wishes should be obeyed, I found that I could not convey all that I meant or make myself understood by everyone whom I wished to understand me. So my memory prompted me. I noticed that people would name some object and then turn towards whatever it was that they had named. I watched them and understood that the sound they made when they wanted to indicate that particular thing was the name which they gave to it, and their actions clearly showed what they meant, for there is a kind of universal language, consisting of expressions of the face and eyes, gestures and tones of voice, which can show whether a person means to ask for something and get it, or refuse it and have nothing to do with it. So, by hearing words arranged in various phrases and constantly repeated, I gradually pieced together what they stood for, and when my tongue had mastered the pronunciation, I began to express my wishes by means of them. In this way I made my wants known to my family and they made theirs known to me, and I took a further step into the stormy life of human society, although I was still subject to the authority of my parents and the will of my elders.

9

But, O God my God, I now went through a period of suffering and humiliation. I was told that it was right and proper for me as a boy to pay attention to my teachers, so that I should do well at my study of grammar and get on in the world. This was the way to gain the respect of others and win for myself what passes for wealth in this world. So I was sent to school to learn to read. I was too small to understand what purpose it might serve and yet, if I was idle at my studies, I was beaten for it, because beating was favoured by tradition. Countless boys long since forgotten had built up this stony path for us to tread and we were made to pass along it, adding to the toil and sorrow of the sons of Adam.

But we found that some men prayed to you, Lord, and we learned from them to do the same, thinking of you in the only way that we could understand, as some great person who could listen to us and help us, even though we could not see you or hear you or touch you. I was still a boy when I first began to pray to you, my Help and Refuge. I used to prattle away to you, and though I was small, my devotion was great when I begged you not to let me be beaten at school. Sometimes, for my own good, you did not grant my prayer, and then my elders and even my parents, who certainly wished me no harm, would laugh at the beating I got— and in those days beatings were my one great bugbear.

O Lord, throughout the world men beseech you to preserve them from the rack and the hook and various similar tortures which terrify them. Some people are merely callous, but if a man clings to you with great devotion, how can his piety inspire him to find it in his heart to make light of these tortures, when he loves those who dread them so fearfully? And yet this was how our parents scoffed at the torments which we boys suffered at the hands of our masters. For we feared the whip just as much as others fear the rack, and we, no less than they, begged you to preserve us from it. But we sinned by reading and writing and studying less than was expected of us. We lacked neither memory nor intelligence, because by your will, O Lord, we had as much of both as was sufficient for our years. But we enjoyed playing games and were punished for them by men who played games themselves. However, grown-up games are known as 'business', and even though boys' games are much the same, they are punished for them by their elders. No one pities either the boys or the men, though surely we deserved pity, for I cannot believe that a good judge would approve of the beatings I received as a boy on the ground that my games delayed my progress in studying subjects which would enable me to play a less creditable game later in life. Was the master who beat me himself very different from me? If he were worsted by a colleague in some petty argument, he would be convulsed with anger and envy, much more so than I was when a playmate beat me at a game of ball.

10

And yet I sinned, O Lord my God, creator and arbiter of all natural things, but arbiter only, not creator, of sin. I sinned, O Lord, by disobeying my parents and the masters of whom I have spoken. For, whatever purpose they had in mind, later on I might have put to good use all the things which they wanted me to learn. I was disobedient, not because I chose something better than they proposed to me, but simply from the love of games. For I liked to score a fine win at sport or to have my ears tickled by the make-believe of the stage, which only made them itch the more. As time went on my eyes shone more and more with the same eager curiosity, because I wanted to see the shows and sports which grown-ups enjoyed. The patrons who pay for the production of these shows are held in esteem such as most parents would wish for their children. Yet the same parents willingly allow their children to be flogged if they are distracted by these displays from the studies which are supposed to fit them to grow rich and give the same sort of shows themselves. Look on these things with pity, O Lord, and free us who now call upon you from such delusions. Set free also those who have not yet called upon you, so that they may pray to you and you may free them from this folly.

11

While still a boy I had been told of the eternal life promised to us by Our Lord, who humbled himself and came down amongst us proud sinners. As a catechumen, I was blessed regularly from birth with the sign of the Cross and was seasoned with God's salt, for, O Lord, my mother placed great hope in you. Once as a child I was taken suddenly ill with a disorder of the stomach and was on the point of death. You, my God, were my guardian even then, and you saw the fervour and strength of my faith as I appealled to the piety of my own mother and to the mother of us all, your Church, to give me the baptism of Christ your Son, who is my God and my Master. My earthly mother was deeply anxious, because in the pure faith of her heart, she was in greater labour to ensure my eternal salvation than she had been at my birth. Had I not quickly recovered, she would have hastened to see that I was admitted to the sacraments of salvation and washed clean by acknowledging you, Lord Jesus, for the pardon of my sins. So my washing in the waters of baptism was postponed, in the surmise that, if I continued to live, I should defile myself again with sin and, after baptism, the guilt of pollution would be greater and more dangerous. Even at that age I already believed in you, and so did my mother and the whole household except for my father. But, in my heart, he did not gain the better of my mother's piety and prevent me from believing in Christ just because he still disbelieved himself. For she did all that she could to see that you, my God, should be a Father to me rather than he. In this you helped her to turn the scales against her husband, whom she always obeyed because by obeying him she obeyed your law, thereby showing greater virtue than he did.

I ask you, my God—for, if it is your will, I long to

know—for what purpose was my baptism postponed at that time? Was it for my good that the reins which held me from sin were slackened? Or is it untrue that they were slackened? If not, why do we continually hear people say, even nowadays, 'Leave him alone and let him do it. He is not yet baptized'? Yet when the health of the body is at stake, no one says 'Let him get worse. He is not yet cured.' It would, then, have been much better if I had been healed at once and if all that I and my family could do had been done to make sure that once my soul had received its salvation, its safety should be left in your keeping, since its salvation had come from you. This would surely have been the better course. But my mother well knew how many great tides of temptation threatened me before I grew up, and she chose to let them beat upon the as yet unmoulded clay rather than upon the finished image which had received the stamp of baptism.

12

These temptations were thought to be less of a danger in boyhood than in adolescence. But even as a boy I did not care for lessons and I disliked being forced to study. All the same I was compelled to learn and good came to me as a result, although it was not of my own making. For I would not have studied at all if I had not been obliged to do so, and what a person does against his will is not to his own credit, even if what he does is good in itself. Nor was the good which came of it due to those who compelled me to study, but to you, my God. For they had not the insight to see that I might put the lessons which they forced me to learn to any other purpose than the satisfaction of man's insatiable desire for the poverty he calls wealth and the infamy he knows as fame. But you, who take every hair of our heads into your reckoning, used for my benefit the mistaken ideas of all those who insisted on making me study; and you used the mistake I made myself, in not wishing to study, as a punishment which I deserved to pay, for I was a great sinner for so small a boy. In this way you turned their faults to my advantage and justly punished me for my own. For this is what you have ordained and so it is with us, that every soul that sins brings its own punishment upon itself.

13

Even now I cannot fully understand why the Greek language, which I learned as a child, was so distasteful to me. I loved Latin, not the elementary lessons but those which I studied later under teachers of literature.

The first lessons in Latin were reading, writing, and counting, and they were as much of an irksome imposition as any studies in Greek. But this, too, was due to the sinfulness and vanity of life, since I was flesh and blood, no better than a breath of wind that passes by and never returns. For these elementary lessons were far more valuable than those which followed, because the subjects were practical. They gave me the power, which I still have, of reading whatever is set before me and writing whatever I wish to write. But in the later lessons I was obliged to memorize the wanderings of a hero named Aeneas, while in the meantime I failed to remember my own erratic ways. I learned to lament the death of Dido, who killed herself for love, while all the time, in the midst of these things, I was dying, separated from you, my God and my Life, and I shed no tears for my own plight.

What can be more pitiful than an unhappy wretch unaware of his own sorry state, bewailing the fate of Dido, who died for love of Aeneas, yet shedding no tears for himself as he dies for want of loving you? O God, you are the Light of my heart, the Bread of my inmost soul, and the Power that weds my mind and the thoughts of my heart. But I did not love you. I broke my troth with you and embraced another while applause echoed about me. For to love this world is to break troth with you, yet men applaud and are ashamed to be otherwise. I did not weep over this, but instead I wept for Dido, who surrendered her life to the sword, while I forsook you and surrendered myself to the lowest of your created things. And if I were forbidden to read these books, I was sad not to be able to read the very things that made me sad. Such folly is held to be a higher and more fruitful form of study than learning to read and write.

But now, my God, let your voice ring in my soul and let your truth proclaim to me that it is wrong to think this. Tell me that reading and writing are by far the better study. This must be true, for I would rather forget the wanderings of Aeneas and all that goes with them, than how to read and write. It is true that curtains are hung over the entrances to the schools where literature is taught, but they are not so much symbols in honour of mystery as veils concealing error. The schoolmasters need not exclaim at my words, for I no longer go in fear of them now that I confess my soul's desires to you, my God, and gladly blame myself for my evil ways so that I may enjoy the good ways you have shown me. Neither those who traffic in literature nor those who buy their wares need exclaim against me. For if I put to them the question whether it is true, as the poet says, that Aeneas once came to Carthage, the less learned will plead ignorance and the better informed will admit that it is not true. But if I ask how the name of Aeneas is spelt, anyone who has learnt to read will give me the right answer, based on the agreed convention which fixes the alphabet for all of us. If I next ask them whether a man would lose more by forgetting how to read and write or by forgetting the fancies dreamed up by the poets, surely everyone who is not out of his wits can see the answer they would give. So it was wrong of me as a boy to prefer empty romances to more valuable studies. In fact it would be truer to say that I loved the one and hated the other. But in those days 'one and one are two, two and two are four' was a loathsome jingle, while the wooden horse and its crew of soldiers, the burning of Troy and even the ghost of Creusa made a most enchanting dream, futile though it was.

14

If this was so, why did I dislike Greek literature, which tells these tales, as much as the Greek language itself? Homer, as well as Virgil, was a skilful spinner of yarns and he is most delightfully imaginative. Nevertheless, as a boy, I found him little to my taste. I suppose that Greek boys think the same about Virgil when they are forced to study him as I was forced to study Homer. There was of course the difficulty which is found in learning any foreign language, and this soured the sweetness of the Greek romances. For I understood not a single word and I was constantly subjected to violent threats and cruel punishments to make me learn. As a baby, of course, I knew no Latin either, but I learned it without fear and fret, simply by keeping my ears open while my nurses fondled me and everyone laughed and played happily with me. I learned it without being forced by threats of punishment, because it was my own wish to be able to give expression to my thoughts. I could never have done this if I had not learnt a few words, not from schoolmasters, but from people who spoke to me and listened when I delivered to their ears whatever thoughts I had conceived. This clearly shows that we learn better in a free spirit of curiosity than under fear and compulsion. But your law, O God, permits the free flow of curiosity to be stemmed by force. From the schoolmaster's cane to the ordeals of martyrdom, your law prescribes bitter medicine to retrieve us from the noxious pleasures which cause us to desert you.

15

Grant my prayer, O Lord, and do not allow my soul to wilt under the discipline which you prescribe. Let me not tire of thanking you for your mercy in rescuing me from all my wicked ways, so that you may be sweeter to me than all the joys which used to tempt me; so that I may love you most intensely and clasp your hand with all the power of my devotion; so that you may save me from all temptation until the end of my days.

You, O Lord, are my King and my God, and in your service I want to use whatever good I learned as a boy. I can speak and write, read and count, and I want these things to be used to serve you, because when I studied other subjects you checked me and forgave me the sins I committed by taking pleasure in such worthless things. It is true that these studies taught me many useful words, but the same words can be learnt by studying something that matters, and this is the safe course for a boy to follow.

16

But we are carried away by custom to our own undoing and it is hard to struggle against the stream. Will this torrent never dry up? How much longer will it sweep the sons of Adam down to that vast and terrible sea which cannot easily be passed, even by those who climb upon the ark of the Cross?

This traditional education taught me that Jupiter

punishes the wicked with his thunderbolts and yet commits adultery himself. The two roles are quite incompatible. All the same he is represented in this way, and the result is that those who follow his example in adultery can put a bold face on it by making false pretences of thunder. But can any schoolmaster in his gown listen unperturbed to a man who challenges him on his own ground and says 'Homer invented these stories and attributed human sins to the gods. He would have done better to provide men with examples of divine goodness'? It would be nearer the truth to say that Homer certainly invented the tales but peopled them with wicked human characters in the guise of gods. In this way their wickedness would not be reckoned a crime, and all who did as they did could be shown to follow the example of the heavenly gods, not that of sinful mortals.

And yet human children are pitched into this hellish torrent, together with the fees which are paid to have them taught lessons like these. Much business is at stake, too, when these matters are publicly debated, because the law decrees that teachers should be paid a salary in addition to the fees paid by their pupils. And the roar of the torrent beating upon its boulders seems to say 'This is the school where men are made masters of words. This is where they learn the art of persuasion, so necessary in business and debate'—as much as to say that, but for a certain passage in Terence, we should never have heard of words like 'shower', 'golden', 'lap', 'deception', 'sky', and the other words which occur in the same scene. Terence brings on to the stage a dissolute youth who excuses his own fornication by pointing to the example of Jupiter. He looks at a picture painted on the wall, which 'shows how Jupiter is said to have deceived the girl Danae by raining a golden shower into her lap'. These are the words with which he incites himself to lechery, as though he had heavenly authority for it: 'What a god he is! His mighty thunder rocks the sky from end to end. You may say that I am only a man, and thundering is beyond my power. But I played the rest of the part well enough, and willingly too'!

The words are certainly not learnt any the more easily by reason of the filthy moral, but filth is committed with greater confidence as a result of learning the words. I have nothing against the words themselves. They are like choice and costly glasses, but they contain the wine of error which had already gone to the heads of the teachers who poured it out for us to drink. If we refused to drink, we were beaten for it, without the right to appeal to a sober judge. With your eyes upon me, my God, my memory can safely recall those days. But it is true that I learned all these things gladly and took a sinful pleasure in them. And for this very reason I was called a promising boy.

17

Let me tell you, my God, how I squandered the brains you gave me on foolish delusions. I was set a task which troubled me greatly, for if I were successful, I might win some praise: if not, I was afraid of disgrace or a beating. I had to recite the speech of Juno, who was pained and angry because she could not prevent Aeneas from sailing to Italy. I had been told that Juno had never really spoken the words, but we were compelled to make believe and follow the flight of the poet's fancy by repeating in prose what he had said in verse. The contest was to be won by the boy who found the best words to suit the meaning and best expressed feelings of sorrow and anger appropriate to the majesty of the character he impersonated.

What did all this matter to me, my God, my true Life? Why did my recitation win more praise than those of the many other boys in my class? Surely it was all so much smoke without fire? Was there no other subject on which I might have sharpened my wits and my tongue? I might have used them, O Lord, to praise you in the words of your Scriptures, which could have been a prop to support my heart, as if it were a young vine, so that it would not have produced this crop of worthless fruit, fit only for the birds to peck at. For offerings can be made to those birds of prey, the fallen angels, in more ways than one.

18

But was it surprising that I was lured into these fruitless pastimes and wandered away from you, my God? I was expected to model myself upon men who were disconcerted by the rebukes they received if they used outlandish words or strange idioms to tell of some quite harmless thing they might have done, but revelled in the applause they earned for the fine flow of well-ordered and nicely balanced phrases with which they described their own acts of indecency. You see all these things, Lord, and yet you keep silence, because you are patient and full of compassion and can tell no lie. Will you be silent for ever? This very day you are ready to rescue from this fearsome abyss any soul that searches for you, any man who says from the depths of his heart, I have eyes only for you; I long, Lord, for your presence; for the soul that is blinded by wicked passions is far from you and cannot see your face. The path that leads us away from you and brings us back again is not measured by footsteps or milestones. The prodigal son of the Scriptures went to live in a distant land to waste in dissipation all the wealth which his father had given him when he set out. But, to reach that land, he did not hire horses, carriages, or ships; he did not take to the air on real wings or set one foot before the other. For you were the Father who gave him riches. You loved him when he set out and you loved him still more when he came home without a penny. But he set his heart on pleasure and his soul was blinded, and this blindness was the measure of the distance he travelled away from you, so that he could not see your face.

O Lord my God, be patient, as you always are, with the men of this world as you watch them and see how strictly they obey the rules of grammar which have been handed down to them, and yet ignore the eternal rules of everlasting salvation which they have received from you. A man who has learnt the traditional rules of pronunciation, or teaches them to others, gives greater scandal if he breaks them by dropping the aitch from 'human being' than if he breaks your rules and hates another human, his fellow man. This is just as perverse as to imagine that our enemies can do us more harm than we do to ourselves by hating them, or that by persecuting another man we can damage him more fatally than we damage our own hearts in the process.

O God, alone in majesty, high in the silence of heaven, unseen by man! we can see how your unremitting justice punishes unlawful ambition with blindness, for a man who longs for fame as a fine speaker will stand up before a human judge, surrounded by a human audience, and lash his opponent with malicious invective, taking the greatest care not to say ' 'uman' instead of 'human' by a slip of the tongue, and yet the thought that the frenzy in his own mind may condemn a human being to death disturbs him not at all.

19

It was at the threshold of a world such as this that I stood in peril as a boy. I was already being prepared for its tournaments by a training which taught me to have a horror of faulty grammar instead of teaching me, when I committed these faults, not to envy others who avoided them. All this, my God, I admit and confess to you. By these means I won praise from the people whose favour I sought, for I thought that the right way to live was to do as they wished. I was blind to the whirlpool of debasement in which I had been plunged away from the sight of your eyes. For in your eyes nothing could be more debased than I was then, since I was even troublesome to the people whom I set out to please. Many and many a time I lied to my tutor, my masters, and my parents, and deceived them because I wanted to play games or watch some futile show or was impatient to imitate what I saw on the stage. I even stole from my parents' larder and from their table, either from greed or to get something to give to other boys in exchange for their favourite toys, which they were willing to barter with me. And in the games I played with them I often cheated in order to come off the better, simply because a vain desire to win had got the better of me. And yet there was nothing I could less easily endure, nothing that made me quarrel more bitterly, than to find others cheating me as I cheated them. All the same, if they found me out and blamed me for it, I would lose my temper rather than give in.

Can this be the innocence of childhood? Far from it, O Lord! But I beg you to forgive it. For commanders and kings may take the place of tutors and schoolmasters, nuts and balls and pet birds may give way to money and estates and servants, but these same passions remain with us while one stage of life follows upon another, just as more severe punishments follow upon the schoolmaster's cane. It was, then, simply because they are small that you used children to symbolize humility when, as our King, you commended it by saying that the kingdom of heaven belongs to such as these.

And yet, Lord, even if you had willed that I should not survive my childhood, I should have owed you gratitude, because you are our God, the supreme Good, the Creator and Ruler of the universe. For even as a child I existed, I was alive, I had the power of feeling; I had an instinct to keep myself safe and sound, to preserve my own being, which was a trace of the single unseen Being from whom it was derived; I had an inner sense which watched over my bodily senses and kept them in full vigour; and even in the small things which occupied my thoughts I found pleasure in the truth. I disliked finding myself in the wrong; my memory was good; I was acquiring the command of words; I enjoyed the company of friends; and I shrank from pain, ignorance, and sorrow. Should I not be grateful that so small a creature possessed such wonderful qualities? But they were all gifts from God, for I did not give them to myself. His gifts are good and the sum of them all is my own self. Therefore, the God who made me must be good and all the good in me is his. I thank him and praise him for all the good in my life, even my life as a boy. But my sin was this, that I looked for pleasure, beauty, and truth not in him but in myself and his other creatures, and the search led me instead to pain, confusion, and error. My God, in whom is my delight, my glory, and my trust, I thank you for your gifts and beg you to preserve and keep them for me. Keep me, too, and so your gifts will grow and reach perfection and I shall be with you myself, for I should not even exist if it were not by your gift.

Book II

1

I must now carry my thoughts back to the abominable things I did in those days, the sins of the flesh which defiled my soul. I do this, my God, not because I love those sins, but so that I may love you. For love of your love I shall retrace my wicked ways. The memory is bitter, but it will help me to savour your sweetness, the sweetness that does not deceive but brings real joy and never fails. For love of your love I shall retrieve myself from the havoc of disruption which tore me to pieces when I turned away from you, whom alone I should have sought, and lost myself instead on many a different quest. For as I grew to manhood I was inflamed with desire for a surfeit of hell's pleasures. Foolhardy as I was, I ran wild with lust that was manifold and rank. In your eyes my beauty vanished and I was foul to the core, yet I was pleased with my own condition and anxious to be pleasing in the eyes of men.

I cared for nothing but to love and be loved. But my love went beyond the affection of one mind for another, beyond the arc of the bright beam of friendship. Bodily desire, like a morass, and adolescent sex welling up within me exuded mists which clouded over and obscured my heart, so that I could not extinguish the clear light of true love from the murk of lust. Love and lust together seethed within me. In my tender youth they swept me away over the precipice of my body's appetites and plunged me in the whirlpool of sin. More and more I angered you, unawares. For I had been deafened by the clank of my chains, the fetters of the death which was my due to punish the pride in my soul. I strayed still farther from you and you did not restrain me. I was tossed and spilled, floundering in the broiling sea of my fornication, and you said no word. How long it was before I learned that you were my true joy! You were silent then, and I went on my way, farther and farther from you, proud in my distress and restless in fatigue, sowing more and more seeds whose only crop was grief.

Was there no one to lull my distress, to turn the fleeting beauty of these new-found attractions to good purpose and set up a goal for their charms, so that the high tide of my youth might have rolled in upon the shore of marriage? The surge might have been calmed and contented by the procreation of children, which is the purpose of marriage, as your law prescribes, O Lord. By this means you form the offspring of our fallen nature, and with a gentle hand you prune back the thorns that have no place in your paradise. For your almighty power is not far from us, even when we are far from you. Or, again, I might have listened more attentively to your voice from the clouds, saying of those who marry that they will meet with outward distress, but I leave you your freedom, that a man does well to abstain from all commerce with women, and that he who is unmarried is concerned with God's claim, asking how he is to please God; whereas the married man is concerned with the world's claim, asking how he is to please his wife. These were the words to which I should have listened with more care, and if I had made myself a eunuch for love of the kingdom of heaven, I should have awaited your embrace with all the greater joy.

But, instead, I was in a ferment of wickedness. I deserted you and allowed myself to be carried away by the sweep of the tide. I broke all your lawful bounds and did not escape your lash. For what man can escape it? You were always present, angry and merciful at once, strewing the pangs of bitterness over all my lawless pleasures to lead me on to look for others unallied with pain. You meant me to find them nowhere but in yourself, O Lord, for you teach us by inflicting pain, you smite so that you may heal, and you kill us so that we may not die away from you. Where was I then and how far was I banished from the bliss of your house in that sixteenth year of my life? This was the age at which the frenzy gripped me and I surrendered myself entirely to lust, which your law forbids but human hearts are not ashamed to sanction. My family made no effort to save me from my fall by marriage. Their only concern was that I should learn how to make a good speech and how to persuade others by my words.

3

In the same year my studies were interrupted. I had already begun to go to the near-by town of Madaura to study literature and the art of public speaking, but I was brought back home while my father, a modest citizen of Thasgaste whose determination was greater than his means, saved up the money to send me farther afield to Carthage. I need not tell all this to you, my God, but in your presence I tell it to my own kind, to those other men, however few, who may perhaps pick up this book. And I tell it so that I and all who read my words may realize the depths from which we are to cry to you. Your ears will surely listen to the cry of a penitent heart which lives the life of faith.

No one had anything but praise for my father who, despite his slender resources, was ready to provide his son with all that was needed to enable him to travel so far for the purpose of study. Many of our townsmen, far richer than my father, went to no such trouble for their children's sake. Yet this same father of mine took no trouble at all to see how I was growing in your sight or whether I was chaste or not. He cared only that I should have a fertile tongue, leaving my heart to bear none of your fruits, my God, though you are the only Master, true and good, of its husbandry.

In the meanwhile, during my sixteenth year, the narrow means of my family obliged me to leave school and live idly at home with my parents. The brambles of lust grew high above my head and there was no one to root them out, certainly not my father. One day at the public baths he saw the signs of active virility coming to life in me and this was enough to make him relish the thought of having grandchildren. He was happy to tell my mother about it, for his happiness was due to the intoxication which causes the world to forget you, its Creator, and to love the things you have created instead of loving you, because the world is drunk with the invisible wine of its own perverted, earthbound will. But in my mother's heart you had already begun

41

to build your temple and laid the foundations of your holy dwelling, while my father was still a catechumen and a new one at that. So, in her piety, she became alarmed and apprehensive, and although I had not yet been baptized, she began to dread that I might follow in the crooked path of those who do not keep their eyes on you but turn their backs instead.

How presumptuous it was of me to say that you were silent, my God, when I drifted farther and farther away from you! Can it be true that you said nothing to me at that time? Surely the words which rang in my ears, spoken by your faithful servant, my mother, could have come from none but you? Yet none of them sank into my heart to make me do as you said. I well remember what her wishes were and how she most earnestly warned me not to commit fornication and above all not to seduce any man's wife. It all seemed woman-ish advice to me and I should have blushed to accept it. Yet the words were yours, though I did not know it. I thought that you were silent and that she was speaking, but all the while you were speaking to me through her, and when I disregarded her, your handmaid, I was disregarding you, though I was both her son and your servant. But I did this unawares and continued head-long on my way. I was so blind to the truth that among my companions I was ashamed to be less disolute than they were. For I heard them bragging of their depravity, and the greater the sin the more they gloried in it, so that I took pleasure in the same vices not only for the enjoyment of what I did, but also for the applause I won.

Nothing deserves to be despised more than vice; yet I gave in more and more to vice simply in order not to be despised. If I had not sinned enough to rival other sinners, I used to pretend that I had done things I had not done at all, because I was afraid that innocence would be taken for cowardice and chastity for weakness. These were the companions with whom I walked the streets of Babylon. I wallowed in its mire as if it were made of spices and precious ointments, and to fix me all the faster in the very depths of sin the unseen enemy trod me underfoot and enticed me to himself, because I was an easy prey for his seductions. For even my mother, who by now had escaped from the centre of Babylon, though she still loitered in its outskirts, did not act upon what she had heard about me from her husband with the same earnestness as she had advised me about chastity. She saw that I was already infected with a disease that would become dangerous later on, but if the growth of my passions could not be cut back to the quick, she did not think it right to restrict them to the bounds of married love. This was because she was afraid that the bonds of marriage might be a hindrance to my hopes for the future—not of course the hope of the life to come, which she reposed in you, but my hopes of success at my studies. Both my parents were unduly eager for me to learn, my father because he gave next to no thought to you and only shallow thought to me, and my mother because she thought that the usual course of study would certainly not hinder me, but would even help me, in my approach to you. To the best of my memory this is how I construe the characters of my parents. Furthermore, I was given a free rein to amuse myself beyond the strict limits of discipline, so that I lost myself in many kinds of evil ways, in all of which a pall of darkness hung between me and the bright light of your truth, my God. What malice proceeded from my pampered heart!

4

It is certain, O Lord, that theft is punished by your law, the law that is written in men's hearts and cannot be erased however sinful they are. For no thief can bear that another thief should steal from him, even if he is rich and the other is driven to it by want. Yet I was willing to steal, and steal I did, although I was not compelled by any lack, unless it were the lack of a sense of justice or a distaste for what was right and a greedy love of doing wrong. For of what I stole I already had plenty, and much better at that, and I had no wish to enjoy the things I coveted by stealing, but only to enjoy the theft itself and the sin. There was a pear-tree near our vineyard, loaded with fruit that was attractive neither to look at nor to taste. Late one night a band of ruffians, myself included, went off to shake down the fruit and carry it away, for we had continued our games out of doors until well after dark, as was our pernicious habit. We took away an enormous quantity of pears, not to eat them ourselves, but simply to throw them to the pigs. Perhaps we ate some of them, but our real pleasure consisted in doing something that was forbidden.

Look into my heart, O God, the same heart on which you took pity when it was in the depths of the abyss. Let my heart now tell you what prompted me to do wrong for no purpose, and why it was only my own love of mischief that made me do it. The evil in me was foul, but I loved it. I loved my own perdition and my own faults, not the things for which I committed wrong, but the wrong itself. My soul was vicious and broke away from your safe keeping to seek its own destruction, looking for no profit in disgrace but only for disgrace itself.

45

5

The eye is attracted by beautiful objects, by gold and silver and all such things. There is great pleasure, too, in feeling something agreeable to the touch, and material things have various qualities to please each of the other senses. Again, it is gratifying to be held in esteem by other men and to have the power of giving them orders and gaining the mastery over them. This is also the reason why revenge is sweet. But our ambition to obtain all these things must not lead us astray from you, O Lord, nor must we depart from what your law allows. The life we live on earth has its own attractions as well, because it has a certain beauty of its own in harmony with all the rest of this world's beauty. Friendship among men, too, is a delightful bond, uniting many souls in one. All these things and their like can be occasions of sin because, good though they are, they are of the lowest order of good, and if we are too much tempted by them we abandon those higher and better things, your truth, your law, and you yourself, O Lord our God. For these earthly things, too, can give joy, though not such joy as my God, who made them all, can give, because honest men will rejoice in the Lord; upright hearts will not boast in vain.

When there is an inquiry to discover why a crime has been committed, normally no one is satisfied until it has been shown that the motive might have been either the desire of gaining, or the fear of losing, one of those good things which I said were of the lowest order. For such things are attractive and have beauty, although they are paltry trifles in comparison with the worth of God's blessed treasures. A man commits murder and we ask the reason. He did it because he wanted his victim's wife or estates for himself, or so that he might live on the proceeds of robbery, or because he was afraid that the other might defraud him of something, or because he had been wronged and was burning for revenge. Surely no one would believe that he would commit murder for no reason but the sheer delight of killing? Sallust tells us that Catiline was a man of insane ferocity, 'who chose to be cruel and vicious without apparent reason'; but we are also told that his purpose was 'not to allow his men to lose heart or waste their skill through lack of practice.' If we ask the reason for this, it is obvious that he meant that once he had made himself master of the government by means of this continual violence, he would obtain honour, power, and wealth and would no longer go in fear of the law because of his crimes or have to face difficulties through lack of funds. So even Catiline did not love crime for crime's sake. He loved something quite different, for the sake of which he committed his crimes.

If the crime of theft which I committed that night as a boy of sixteen were a living thing, I could speak to it and ask what it was that, to my shame, I loved in it. I had no beauty because it was a robbery. It is true that the pears which we stole had beauty, because they were created by you, the good God, who are the most beautiful of all beings and the Creator of all things, the supreme Good and my own true Good. But it was not the pears that my unhappy soul desired. I had plenty of my own, better than those, and I only picked them so that I might steal. For no sooner had I picked them than I threw them away, and tasted nothing in them but my own sin, which I relished and enjoyed. If any part of one of those pears passed my lips, it was the sin that gave it flavour.

And now, O Lord my God, now that I ask what pleasure I had in that theft, I find that it had no beauty to attract me. I do not mean beauty of the sort that justice and prudence possess, nor the beauty that is in man's mind and in his memory and in the life that animates him, nor the beauty of the stars in their allotted places or of the earth and sea, teeming with new life born to replace the old as it passes away. It did not even have the shadowy, deceptive beauty which makes vice attractive—pride, for instance, which is a pretence of superiority, imitating yours, for you alone are God, supreme over all; or ambition, which is only a craving for honour and glory, when you alone are to be honoured before all and you alone are glorious for ever. Cruelty is the weapon of the powerful, used to make others fear them: yet no one is to be feared but God alone, from whose power nothing can be snatched away or stolen by any man at any time or place or by any means. The lustful use caresses to win the love they crave for, yet no caress is sweeter than your charity and no love is more rewarding than the love of your truth, which shines in beauty above all else. Inquisitiveness has all the appearance of a thirst for knowledge, yet you have supreme knowledge of all things. Ignorance, too, and stupidity choose to go under the mask of simplicity and innocence, because you are simplicity itself and no innocence is greater than yours. You are innocent even of the harm which overtakes the wicked, for it is the result of their own actions. Sloth poses as the love of peace: yet what certain peace is there besides the Lord? Extravagance masquerades as fullness and abundance: but you are the full, unfailing store of never-dying sweetness. The spendthrift makes a pretence of liberality: but you are the most generous dispenser of all good. The covetous want many possessions for themselves: you possess all. The envious struggle for preferment: but what is to be preferred before you? Anger demands revenge: but what vengeance is as just as yours? Fear shrinks from any sudden, unwonted danger which threatens the things that it loves, for its only care is safety: but to you nothing is strange, nothing unforeseen. No one can part you from the things that you love, and safety is assured nowhere but in you. Grief eats away its heart for the loss of things which it took pleasure in desiring, because it wants to be like you, from whom nothing can be taken away.

So the soul defiles itself with unchaste love when it turns away from you and looks elsewhere for things which it cannot find pure and unsullied except by returning to you. All who desert you and set themselves up against you merely copy you in a perverse way; but by this very act of imitation they only show that you are the Creator of all nature and, consequently, that there is no place whatever where man may hide away from you.

What was it, then, that pleased me in that act of theft? Which of my Lord's powers did I imitate in a perverse and wicked way? Since I had no real power to break his law, was it that I enjoyed at least the pretence of doing so, like a prisoner who creates for himself the illusion of liberty by doing something wrong, when he has no fear of punishment, under a feeble hallucination of power? Here was the slave who ran away from his master and chased a shadow instead! What an abomination! What a parody of life! What abysmal death! Could I enjoy doing wrong for no other reason than that it was wrong?

7

What return shall I make to the Lord for my ability to recall these things with no fear in my soul? I will love you, Lord, and thank you, and praise your name, because you have forgiven me such great sins and such wicked deeds. I acknowledge that it was by your grace and mercy that you melted away my sins like ice. I acknowledge, too, that by your grace I was preserved from whatever sins I did not commit, for there was no knowing what I might have done, since I loved evil even if it served no purpose. I avow that you have forgiven me all, both the sins which I committed of my own accord and those which by your guidance I was spared from committing.

What man who reflects upon his own weakness can dare to claim that his own efforts have made him chaste and free from sin, as though this entitled him to love you the less, on the ground that he had less need of the mercy by which you forgive the sins of the penitent? There are some who have been called by you and because they have listened to your voice they have avoided the sins which I here record and confess for them to read. But let them not deride me for having been cured by the same Doctor who preserved them from sickness, or at least from such grave sickness as mine. Let them love you just as much, or even more, than I do, for they can see that the same healing hand which rid me of the great fever of my sins protects them from falling sick of the same disease.

8

It brought me no happiness, for what harvest did I reap from acts which now make me blush, particularly from that act of theft? I loved nothing in it except the thieving, though I cannot truly speak of that as a 'thing' that I could love, and I was only the more miserable because of it. And yet, as I recall my feelings at the time, I am quite sure that I would not have done it on my own. Was it then that I also enjoyed the company of those with whom I committed the crime? If this is so, there was something else I loved besides the act of theft; but I cannot call it 'something else', because companionship, like theft, is not a thing at all.

No one can tell me the truth of it except my God,

who enlightens my mind and dispels its shadows. What conclusion am I trying to reach from these questions and this discussion? It is true that if the pears which I stole had been to my taste, and if I had wanted to get them for myself, I might have committed the crime on my own if I had needed to do no more than that to win myself the pleasure. I should have had no need to kindle my glowing desire by rubbing shoulders with a gang of accomplices. But as it was not the fruit that gave me pleasure, I must have got it from the crime itself, from the thrill of having partners in sin.

9

How can I explain my mood? It was certainly a very vile frame of mind and one for which I suffered; but how can I account for it? Who knows his own frailties?

We were tickled to laughter by the prank we had played, because no one suspected us of it although the owners were furious. Why was it, then, that I thought it fun not to have been the only culprit? Perhaps it was because we do not easily laugh when we are alone. True enough: but even when a man is all by himself and quite alone, sometimes he cannot help laughing if he thinks or hears or sees something especially funny.

All the same, I am quite sure that I would never have done this thing on my own.

My God, I lay all this before you, for it is still alive in my memory. By myself I would not have committed that robbery. It was not the takings that attracted me but the raid itself, and yet to do it by myself would have been no fun and I should not have done it. This was friendship of a most unfriendly sort, bewitching my mind in an inexplicable way. For the sake of a laugh, a little sport, I was glad to do harm and anxious to damage another; and that without thought of profit for myself or retaliation for injuries received! And all because we are ashamed to hold back when others say 'Come on! Let's do it!'

10

Can anyone unravel this twisted tangle of knots? I shudder to look at it or think of such abomination. I long instead for innocence and justice, graceful and splendid in eyes whose sight is undefiled. My longing fills me and yet it cannot cloy. With them is certain peace and life that cannot be disturbed. The man who enters their domain goes to share the joy of his Lord. He shall know no fear and shall lack no good. In him that is goodness itself he shall find his own best way of life. But I deserted you, my God. In my youth I wandered away, too far from your sustaining hand, and created of myself a barren waste.

Book III

1

I went to Carthage, where I found myself in the midst of a hissing cauldron of lust. I had not yet fallen in love, but I was in love with the idea of it, and this feeling that something was missing made me despise myself for not being more anxious to satisfy the need. I began to look around for some object for my love, since I badly wanted to love something. I had no liking for the safe path without pitfalls, for although my real need was for you, my God, who are the food of the soul, I was not aware of this hunger. I felt no need for the food that does not perish, not because I had had my fill of it, but because the more I was starved of it the less palatable it seemed. Because of this my soul fell sick. It broke out in ulcers and looked about desperately for some material, worldly means of relieving the itch which they caused. But material things, which have no soul, could not be true objects for my love. To love and to have my love returned was my heart's desire, and it would be all the sweeter if I could also enjoy the body of the one who loved me.

So I muddied the stream of friendship with the filth of lewdness and clouded its clear waters with hell's black river of lust. And yet, in spite of this rank depravity, I was vain enough to have ambitions of cutting a fine figure in the world. I also fell in love, which was a snare of my own choosing. My God, my God of mercy, how good you were to me, for you mixed much bitterness in that cup of pleasure! My love was returned and finally shackled me in the bonds of its consummation. In the midst of my joy I was caught up in the coils of trouble, for I was lashed with the cruel, fiery rods of jealousy and suspicion, fear, anger, and quarrels.

2

I was much attracted by the theatre, because the plays reflected my own unhappy plight and were tinder to my fire. Why is it that men enjoy feeling sad at the sight of tragedy and suffering on the stage, although they would be most unhappy if they had to endure the same fate themselves? Yet they watch the plays because they hope to be made to feel sad, and the feeling of sorrow is what they enjoy. What miserable delirium this is! The more a man is subject to such suffering himself, the more easily he is moved by it in the theatre. Yet when he suffers himself, we call it misery: when he suffers out of sympathy with others, we call it pity. But what sort of pity can we really feel for an imaginary scene on the stage? The audience is not called upon to offer help but only to feel sorrow, and the more they are pained the more they applaud the author. Whether this human agony is based on fact or is simply imaginary, if it is acted so badly that the audience is not moved to sorrow, they leave the theatre in a disgruntled and critical mood; whereas, if they are made to feel pain, they stay to the end watching happily.

This shows that sorrow and tears can be enjoyable. Of course, everyone wants to be happy; but even if no one likes being sad, is there just the one exception that, because we enjoy pitying others, we welcome their misfortunes, without which we could not pity them? If so, it is because friendly feelings well up in us like the waters of a spring. But what course do these waters follow? Where do they flow? Why do they trickle away to join that stream of boiling pitch, the hideous flood of lust? For by their own choice they lose themselves and become absorbed in it. They are diverted from their true course and deprived of their original heavenly calm.

Of course this does not mean that we must arm ourselves against compassion. There are times when we must welcome sorrow on behalf of others. But for the sake of our souls we must beware of uncleanness. My God must be the Keeper of my soul, the God of our fathers, who is to be exalted and extolled for ever more. My soul must guard against uncleanness.

I am not nowadays insensible to pity. But in those days I used to share the joy of stage lovers and their sinful pleasure in each other even though it was all done in make-believe for the sake of entertainment; and when they were parted, pity of a sort led me to share their grief. I enjoyed both these emotions equally. But now I feel more pity for a man who is happy in his sins than for one who has to endure the ordeal of forgoing some harmful pleasure or being deprived of some enjoyment which was really an affliction. Of the two, this sort of pity is certainly the more genuine, but the sorrow which it causes is not a source of pleasure. For although a man who is sorry for the sufferings of others deserves praise for his charity, nevertheless, if his pity is genuine, he would prefer that there should be no cause for his sorrow. If the impossible could happen and kindness were unkind, a man whose sense of pity was true and sincere might want others to suffer so that he could pity them. Sorrow may therefore be commendable but never desirable. For it is powerless to stab you, Lord God, and this is why the love you bear for our souls and the compassion you show for them are pure and unalloyed, far purer than the love and pity which we feel ourselves. But who can prove himself worthy of such a calling?

However, in those unhappy days I enjoyed the pangs of sorrow. I always looked for things to wring my heart and the more tears an actor caused me to shed by his performance on the stage, even though he was portraying the imaginary distress of others, the more delightful and attractive I found it. Was it any wonder that I, the unhappy sheep who strayed from your flock, impatient of your shepherding, became infected with a loathsome mange? Hence my love of things which made me sad. I did not seek the kind of sorrow which would wound me deeply, for I had no wish to endure the sufferings which I saw on the stage; but I enjoyed fables and fictions, which could only graze the skin. But where the fingers scratch, the skin becomes inflamed. It swells and festers with hideous pus. And the same happened to me. Could the life I led be called true life, my God?

3

Yet all the while, far above, your mercy hovered faithfully about me. I exhausted myself in depravity, in the pursuit of an unholy curiosity. I deserted you and sank to the bottom-most depths of scepticism and the mockery of devil-worship. My sins were a sacrifice to the devil, and for all of them you chastised me. I defied you even so far as to relish the thought of lust, and gratify it too, within the walls of your church during the celebration of your mysteries. For such a deed I deserved to pluck the fruit of death, and you punished me for it with a heavy lash. But, compared with my guilt, the penalty was nothing. How infinite is your mercy, my God! You are my Refuge from the terrible dangers amongst which I wandered, head on high, intent upon withdrawing still further from you. I loved my own way, not yours, but it was a truant's freedom that I loved.

Besides these pursuits I was also studying for the law. Such ambition was held to be honourable and I determined to succeed in it. The more unscrupulous I was, the greater my reputation was likely to be, for men are so blind that they even take pride in their blindness. By now I was at the top of the school of rhetoric. I was pleased with my superior status and swollen with conceit. All the same, as you well know, Lord, I behaved far more quietly than the 'Wreckers', a title of ferocious devilry which the fashionable set chose for themselves. I had nothing whatever to do with their outbursts of violence, but I lived amongst them, feeling a perverse sense of shame because I was not like them. I kept company with them and there were times when I found their friendship a pleasure, but I always had a horror of what they did when they lived up to their name. Without provocation they would set upon some timid newcomer, gratuitously affronting his sense of decency for their own amusement and using it as fodder for their spiteful jests. This was the devil's own behaviour or not far different. 'Wreckers' was a fit name for them, for they were already adrift and total wrecks themselves. The mockery and trickery which they loved to practise on others was a secret snare of the devil, by which they were mocked and tricked themselves.

4

These were the companions with whom I studied the art of eloquence at that impressionable age. It was my ambition to be a good speaker, for the unhallowed and inane purpose of gratifying human vanity. The prescribed course of study brought me to a work by an author named Cicero, whose writing nearly everyone admires, if not the spirit of it. The title of the book is *Hortensius* and it recommends the reader to study philosophy. It altered my outlook on life. It changed my

63

prayers to you, O Lord, and provided me with new hopes and aspirations. All my empty dreams suddenly lost their charm and my heart began to throb with a bewildering passion for the wisdom of eternal truth. I began to climb out of the depths to which I had sunk, in order to return to you. For I did not use the book as a whetstone to sharpen my tongue. It was not the style of it but the contents which won me over, and yet the allowance which my mother paid me was supposed to be spent on putting an edge on my tongue. I was now in my nineteenth year and she supported me, because my father had died two years before.

My God, how I burned with longing to have wings to carry me back to you, away from all earthly things, although I had no idea what you would do with me! For yours is the wisdom. In Greek the word 'philosophy' means 'love of wisdom', and it was with this love that the *Hortensius* inflamed me. There are people for whom philosophy is a means of misleading others, for they misuse its great name, its attractions, and its integrity to give colour and gloss to their own errors. Most of these so-called philosophers who lived in Cicero's time and before are noted in the book. He shows them up in their true colours and makes quite clear how wholesome is the admonition which the Holy Spirit gives in the words of your good and true servant, Paul: Take care not to let anyone cheat you with his philosophizings, with empty fantasies drawn from human tradition, from worldly principles; they were never Christ's teaching. In Christ the whole plenitude of Deity is embodied and dwells in him.

But, O Light of my heart, you know that at that time, although Paul's words were not known to me, the only thing that pleased me in Cicero's book was his advice not simply to admire one or another of the schools of philosophy, but to love wisdom itself, whatever it might be, and to search for it, pursue it, hold it, and embrace it firmly. These were the words which excited me and set me burning with fire, and the only check to this blaze of enthusiasm was that they made no mention of the name of Christ. For by your mercy, Lord, from the time when my mother fed me at the breast of my infant heart had been suckled dutifully on his name, the name of our Son, my Saviour. Deep inside my heart his name remained, and nothing could entirely captivate me, however learned, however neatly expressed, however true it might be, unless his name were in it.

5

So I made up my mind to examine the holy Scriptures and see what kind of books they were. I discovered something that was at once beyond the understanding of the proud and hidden from the eyes of children. Its gait was humble, but the heights it reached were sublime. It was enfolded in mysteries, and I was not the kind of man to enter into it or bow my head to follow where it led. But these were not the feelings I had when I first read the Scriptures. To me they seemed quite unworthy of comparison with the stately prose of Cicero, because I had too much conceit to accept their simplicity and not enough insight to penetrate their depths. It is surely true that as the child grows these books grow with him. But I was too proud to call myself a child. I was inflated with self-esteem, which made me think myself a great man.

6

I fell in with a set of sensualists, men with glib tongues who ranted and raved and had the snares of the devil in their mouths. They baited the traps by confusing the syllables of the names of God the Father, God the Son Our Lord Jesus Christ, and God the Holy Ghost, the Paraclete, who comforts us. These names were always on the tips of their tongues, but only as sounds which they mouthed aloud, for in their hearts they had no inkling of the truth. Yet 'Truth and truth alone' was the motto which they repeated to me again and again, although the truth was nowhere to be found in them. All that they said was false, both what they said about you, who truly are the Truth, and what they said about this world and its first principles, which were your creation. But I ought not to have been content with what the philosophers said about such things, even when they spoke the truth. I should have passed beyond them for love of you, my supreme Father, my good Father, in whom all beauty has its source.

Truth! Truth! How the very marrow of my soul within me yearned for it as they dinned it in my ears over and over again! To them it was no more than a name to be voiced or a word to be read in their libraries of huge books. But while my hunger was for you, for Truth itself, these were the dishes on which they served me up the sun and the moon, beautiful works of yours but still only your works, not you yourself nor even the greatest of your created things. For your spiritual works are greater than these material things, however brightly they may shine in the sky.

But my hunger and thirst were not even for the greatest of your works, but for you, my God, because you are Truth itself with whom there can be no change, no swerving from your course. Yet the dishes they set before me were still loaded with dazzling fantasies, illusions with which the eye deceives the mind.

It would have been better to love the sun itself, which at least is real as far as we can see. But I gulped down this food, because I thought that it was you. I had no relish for it, because the taste it left in my mouth was not the taste of truth—it could not be, for it was not you but an empty sham. And it did not nourish me, but starved me all the more. The food we dream of is very like the food we eat when we are awake, but it does not nourish because it is only a dream. Yet the things they gave me to eat were not in the least like you, as now I know since you have spoken to me. They were dream-substances, mock realities, far less true than the real things which we see with the sight of our eyes in the sky or on the earth. These things are seen by bird and beast as well as by ourselves, and they are far more certain than any image we conceive of them. And in turn we can picture them to ourselves with greater certainty than the vaster, infinite things which we surmise from them. Such things have no existence at all, but they were the visionary foods on which I was then fed but not sustained.

But you, O God whom I love and on whom I lean in weakness so that I may be strong, you are not the sun and the moon and the stars, even though we see these bodies in the heavens; nor are you those other bodies which we do not see in the sky, for you created them and, in your reckoning, they are not even among the greatest of your works. How far, then, must you really be from those fantasies of mine, those imaginary material things which do not exist at all! The images we form in our mind's eye, when we picture things that really do exist, are far better founded than these inventions; and the things themselves are still more certain than the images we form of them. But you are not these things. Neither are you the soul, which is the life of bodies and, since it gives them life, must be better and more certain than they are themselves. But you are the life of souls, the life of lives. You live, O Life of my soul, because you are life itself, immutable.

Where were you in those days? How far away from me? I was wandering far from you and I was not even allowed to eat the husks on which I fed the swine. For surely the fables of the poets and the penmen are better than the traps which those impostors set! There is certainly more to be gained from verses and poems and tales like the flight of Medea than from their stories of the five elements disguised in various ways because of the five dens of darkness. These things simply do not exist and they are death to those who believe in them. Verses and poems can provide real food for thought, but although I used to recite verses about Medea's flight through the air, I never maintained that they were true; and I never believed the poems which I heard others recite. But I did believe the tales which these men told.

These were the stages of my pitiful fall into the depths of hell, as I struggled and strained for lack of the truth. My God, you had mercy on me even before I had confessed to you; but I now confess that all this was because I tried to find you, not through the understanding of the mind, by which you meant us to be superior to the beasts, but through the senses of the flesh. Yet you were deeper than my inmost understanding and higher than the topmost height that I could reach. I had blundered upon that woman in Solomon's parable who, ignorant and unabashed, sat at her door and said Stolen waters are sweetest, and bread is better eating when there is none to see. She inveigled me because she found me living in the outer world that lay before my eyes, the eyes of the flesh, and dwelling upon the food which they provided for my mind.

7

There is another reality besides this, though I knew nothing of it. My own specious reasoning induced me to give in to the sly arguments of fools who asked me what was the origin of evil, whether God was confined to the limits of a bodily shape, whether he had hair and nails, and whether men could be called just if they had more than one wife at the same time, or killed other men, or sacrificed living animals. My ignorance was so great that these questions troubled me, and while I thought I was approaching the truth, I was only departing the further from it. I did not know that evil is nothing but the removal of good until finally no good remains. How could I see this when with the sight of my eyes I saw no more than material things and with the sight of my mind no more than their images? I did not know that God is a spirit, a being without bulk and without limbs defined in length and breadth. For bulk is less in the part than in the whole, and if it is infinite, it is less in any part of it which can be defined within fixed limits than it is in its infinity. It cannot, therefore, be everywhere entirely whole, as a spirit is and as God is. Nor had I the least notion what it is in us that gives us our being, or what the Scriptures mean when they say that we are made in God's image.

I knew nothing of the true underlying justice which judges, not according to convention, but according to the truly equitable law of Almighty God. This is the law by which each age and place forms rules of conduct best suited to itself, although the law itself is always and everywhere the same and does not differ from place to place or from age to age. I did not see that by the sanction of this law Abraham and Isaac, Jacob, Moses, David, and the others whom God praised were just men, although they have been reckoned sinners by men who are not qualified to judge, for they try them by human standards and assess all the rights and wrongs of the human race by the measure of their own customs. Anyone who does this behaves like a man who knows nothing about armour and cannot tell which piece is meant for which part of the body, so that he tries to cover his head with a shinpiece and fix a helmet on his foot, and then complains because they will not fit; or like a shopkeeper who is allowed to sell his wares in the morning, but grumbles because the afternoon is a public holiday and he is not allowed to trade; or like a man who sees one of the servants in a house handling things which the cellar-man is not allowed to touch, or finds something being done in the stableyard which is not allowed in the diningroom, and is then indignant because the members of the household, living together in one house, are not all given the same privileges in all parts of the house.

The people of whom I am speaking have the same sort of grievance when they hear that things which good men could do without sin in days gone by are not permitted in ours, and that God gave them one commandment and has given us another. He has done this because the times have demanded it, although men were subject to the same justice in those days as we are in these. Yet those who complain about this understand that when we are dealing with a single man, a single day, or a single house, each part of the whole has a different function suited to it. What may be done at one time of day is not allowed at the next, and what may be done, or must be done, in one room is forbidden and punished in another. This does not mean that justice is erratic or variable, but that the times over which it presides are not always the same, for it is the nature of time to change. Man's life on earth is short and he cannot, by his own perception, see the connexion between the conditions of earlier times and of other nations, which he has not experienced himself, and those of his own times, which are familiar to him. But when only one individual, one day, or one house is concerned, he can easily see what is suitable for each part of the whole and for each member of the household, and what must be done at which times and places. These things he accepts: but with the habits of other ages he finds fault.

I knew nothing of this at that time. I was quite unconscious of it, quite blind to it, although it stared me in the face. When I composed verses, I could not fit any foot in any position that I pleased. Each metre was differently scanned and I could not put the same foot in every position in the same line. And yet the art of poetry, by which I composed, does not vary from one line to another: it is the same for all alike. But I did not discern that justice, which those good and holy men obeyed, in a far more perfect and sublime way than poetry contains in itself at one and the same time all the principles which it prescribes, without discrepancy; although, as times change, it prescribes and apportions them, not all at once, but according to the needs of the times. Blind to this, I found fault with the holy patriarchs not only because, in their own day, they acted as God commanded and inspired them, but also because they predicted the future as he revealed it to them.

8

Surely it is never wrong at any time or in any place for a man to love God with his whole heart and his whole soul and his whole mind and to love his neighbour as himself? Sins against nature, therefore, like the sin of Sodom, are abominable and deserve punishment wherever and whenever they are committed. If all nations committed them, all alike would be held guilty of the same charge in God's law, for our Maker did not prescribe that we should use each other in this way. In fact the relationship which we ought to have with God is itself violated when our nature, of which he is the Author, is desecrated by perverted lust.

On the other hand, offences against human codes of conduct vary according to differences of custom, so that no one, whether he is a native or a foreigner, may, to suit his own pleasure, violate the conventions established by the customary usage or the law of the community or the state. For any part that is out of keeping with the whole is at fault. But if God commands a nation to do something contrary to its customs or constitutions, it must be done even if it has never been done in that country before. If it is a practice which has been discontinued, it must be resumed, and if it was not a law before, it must be enacted. In his own kingdom a king has the right to make orders which neither he nor any other has ever made before. Obedience to his orders is not against the common interest of the community; in fact, if they were disobeyed, the common interest would suffer, because it is the general agreement in human communities that the ruler is obeyed. How much more right, then, has God to give commands, since he is the Ruler of all creation and all his creatures must obey his commandments without demur! For all must yield to God just as, in the government of human society, the lesser authority must yield to the greater.

With sins of violence the case is the same as with sins

against nature. Here the impulse is to injure others, either by word or by deed, but by whichever means it is done, there are various reasons for doing it. A man may injure his enemy for the sake of revenge; a robber may assault a traveller to secure for himself something that is not his own; or a man may attack someone whom he fears in order to avoid danger to himself. Or the injury may be done from envy, which will cause an unhappy man to harm another more fortunate than himself or a rich man to harm someone whose rivalry he fears for the future or already resents. Again, it may be done for the sheer joy of seeing others suffer, as is the case with those who watch gladiators or make fun of other people and jeer at them.

These are the main categories of sin. They are hatched from the lust for power, from gratification of the eye, and from gratification of corrupt nature—from one or two of these or from all three together. Because of them, O God most high, most sweet, our lives offend against your ten-stringed harp, your commandments, the three which proclaim our duty to you and the seven which proclaim our duty to men.

But how can sins of vice be against you, since you cannot be marred by perversion? How can sins of violence be against you, since nothing can injure you? Your punishments are for the sins which men commit against themselves, because although they sin against you, they do wrong to their own souls and their malice is self-betrayed. They corrupt and pervert their own nature, which you made and for which you shaped the rules, either by making wrong use of the things which you allow, or by becoming inflamed with passion to make unnatural use of things which you do not allow. Or else their guilt consists in raving against you in their hearts and with their tongues and *kicking against the goad*, or in playing havoc with the restrictions of human society and brazenly exulting in private feuds and factions, each according to his fancies or his fads.

This is what happens, O Fountain of life, when we abandon you, who are the one true Creator of all that ever was or is, and each of us proudly sets his heart on some one part of your creation instead of on the whole. So it is by the path of meekness and devotion that we must return to you. You rid us of our evil habits and forgive our sins when we confess to you. You listen to the groans of the prisoners and free us from the chains which we have forged for ourselves. This you do for us unless we toss our heads against you in the illusion of liberty and in our greed for gain, at the risk of losing all, love our own good better than you yourself, who are the common good of all.

Among these vices and crimes and all the endless ways in which men do wrong there are also the sins of those who follow the right path but go astray. By the rule of perfection these lapses are condemned, if we judge them aright, but the sinners may yet be praised, for they give promise of better fruit to come, like the young shoots which later bear the ears of corn. Sometimes we also do things which have every appearance of being sins against nature or against our fellow men, but are not sins because they offend neither you, the Lord our God, nor the community in which we live. For example, a man may amass a store of goods to meet the needs of life or some contingency, but it does not necessarily follow that he is a miser. Or he may be punished by those whose duty it is to correct misdemeanours, but it is by no means certain that they do it out of wanton cruelty. Many of the things we do may therefore seem wrong to men but are approved in the light of your knowledge, and many which men applaud are condemned in your eyes. This is because the appearance of what we do is often different from the intention with which we do it, and the circumstances at the time may not be clear.

But when you suddenly command us to do something strange and unforeseen, even if you had previously forbidden it, none can doubt that the command must be obeyed, even though, for the time being, you may conceal the reason for it and it may conflict with the established rule of custom in some forms of society; for no society is right and good unless it obeys you. But happy are they who know that the commandment was yours. For all that your servants do is done as an example of what is needed for the present or as a sign of what is yet to come.

10

I was ignorant of this and derided those holy servants and prophets of yours. But all that I achieved by deriding them was to earn your derision for myself, for I was gradually led to believe such nonsense as that a fig wept when it was plucked, and that the tree which bore it shed tears of mother's milk. But if some sanctified member of the sect were to eat the fig—someone else, of course, would have committed the sin of plucking it—he would digest it and breathe it out again in the form of angels or even as particles of God, retching them up as he groaned in prayer. These particles of the true and supreme God were supposed to be imprisoned in the fruit and could only be released by means of the stomach and teeth of one of the elect. I was foolish enough to believe that we should show more kindness to the fruits of the earth than to mankind, for whose use they were intended. If a starving man, not a Manichee, were to beg for a mouthful, they thought it a crime worthy of mortal punishment to give him one.

11

But you sent down your help from above and rescued my soul from the depths of this darkness because my mother, your faithful servant, wept to you for me, shedding more tears for my spiritual death than other mothers shed for the bodily death of a son. For in her faith and in the spirit which she had from you she looked on me as dead. You heard her and did not despise the tears which streamed down and watered the earth in every place where she bowed her head in prayer. You heard her, for how else can I explain the dream with which you consoled her, so that she agreed to live with me and eat at the same table in our home? Lately she had refused to do this, because she loathed and shunned the blasphemy of my false beliefs.

She dreamed that she was standing on a wooden rule, and coming towards her in a halo of splendour she saw a young man who smiled at her in joy, although she herself was sad and quite consumed with grief. He asked her the reason for her sorrow and her daily tears, not because he did not know, but because he had something to tell her, for this is what happens in visions. When she replied that her tears were for the soul I had lost, he told her to take heart for, if she looked carefully, she would see that where she was, there also was I. And when she looked, she saw me standing beside her on the same rule.

Where could this dream have come from, unless it was that you listened to the prayer of her heart? For your goodness is almighty; you take good care of each of us as if you had no others in your care, and you look after all as you look after each. And surely it was for the same reason that, when she told me of the dream and I tried to interpret it as a message that she need not despair of being one day such as I was then, she said at once and without hesitation 'No! He did not say "Where he is, you are", but "Where you are, he is".'

I have often said before and, to the best of my memory, I now declare to you, Lord, that I was much moved by this answer, which you gave me through my mother. She was not disturbed by my interpretation of her dream, plausible though it was, but quickly saw the true meaning, which I had not seen until she spoke. I was more deeply moved by this than by the dream itself, in which the joy for which this devout woman had still so long to wait was foretold so long before to comfort her in the time of her distress. For nearly nine years were yet to come during which I wallowed deep in the mire and the darkness of delusion. Often I tried to lift myself, only to plunge the deeper. Yet all the time this chaste, devout, and prudent woman, a widow such as is close to your heart, never ceased to pray at all hours and to offer you the tears she shed for me. The dream had given new spirit to her hope, but she gave no rest to her sighs and her tears. Her prayers reached your presence and yet you still left me to twist and turn in the dark.

12

I remember that in the meantime you gave her another answer to her prayers, though there is much besides this that escapes my memory and much too that I must omit, because I am in haste to pass on to other things, which I am more anxious to confess to you.

This other answer you gave her through the mouth of one of your priests, a bishop who had lived his life in the Church and was well versed in the Scriptures. My mother asked him, as a favour, to have a talk with me, so that he might refute my errors, drive the evil out of my mind, and replace it with good. He often did this when he found suitable pupils, but he refused to do it for me—a wise decision, as I afterwards realized. He told her that I was still unripe for instruction because, as she had told him, I was brimming over with the novelty of the heresy and had already upset a great many simple people with my casuistry. 'Leave him alone', he said. 'Just pray to God for him. From his own reading he will discover his mistakes and the depth of his profanity.'

At the same time he told her that when he was a child his misguided mother had handed him over to the Manichees. He had not only read almost all their books, but had also made copies of them, and even though no one argued the case with him or put him right, he had seen for himself that he ought to have nothing to do with the sect; and accordingly he had left it. Even after she had heard this my mother still would not be pacified, but persisted all the more with her tears and her entreaties that he should see me and discuss the matter. At last he grew impatient and said

83

'Leave me and go in peace. It cannot be that the son of these tears should be lost.'

In later years, as we talked together, she used to say that she accepted these words as a message from heaven.

PENGUIN 60s CLASSICS

PENGUIN 60s CLASSICS

HENRY JAMES · *The Lesson of the Master*
FRANZ KAFKA · *The Judgement* and *In the Penal Colony*
THOMAS À KEMPIS · *Counsels on the Spiritual Life*
HEINRICH VON KLEIST · *The Marquise of O—*
LIVY · *Hannibal's Crossing of the Alps*
NICCOLÒ MACHIAVELLI · *The Art of War*
SIR THOMAS MALORY · *The Death of King Arthur*
GUY DE MAUPASSANT · *Boule de Suif*
FRIEDRICH NIETZSCHE · *Zarathustra's Discourses*
OVID · *Orpheus in the Underworld*
PLATO · *Phaedrus*
EDGAR ALLAN POE · *The Murders in the Rue Morgue*
ARTHUR RIMBAUD · *A Season in Hell*
JEAN-JACQUES ROUSSEAU · *Meditations of a Solitary Walker*
ROBERT LOUIS STEVENSON · *Dr Jekyll and Mr Hyde*
TACITUS · *Nero and the Burning of Rome*
HENRY DAVID THOREAU · *Civil Disobedience* and *Reading*
LEO TOLSTOY · *The Death of Ivan Ilyich*
IVAN TURGENEV · *Three Sketches from a Hunter's Album*
MARK TWAIN · *The Man That Corrupted Hadleyburg*
GIORGIO VASARI · *Lives of Three Renaissance Artists*
EDITH WHARTON · *Souls Belated*
WALT WHITMAN · *Song of Myself*
OSCAR WILDE · *The Portrait of Mr W. H.*

ANONYMOUS WORKS

Beowulf and Grendel
Buddha's Teachings
Gilgamesh and Enkidu

Krishna's Dialogue on the Soul
Tales of Cú Chulaind
Two Viking Romances

READ MORE IN PENGUIN